The World on Your Plate: 50 Global Recipes

By: Kelly Johnson

Table of Contents

- Moroccan Chicken Tagine
- Italian Margherita Pizza
- Japanese Ramen Bowl
- Mexican Street Tacos
- Indian Butter Chicken
- Greek Moussaka
- French Coq au Vin
- Thai Green Curry
- Korean Bibimbap
- Spanish Paella
- Vietnamese Pho
- Chinese Kung Pao Chicken
- Ethiopian Doro Wat
- Brazilian Feijoada
- Turkish Kebab
- American Barbecue Ribs
- Argentinian Empanadas
- Lebanese Tabouleh
- Swedish Meatballs
- Peruvian Ceviche
- Russian Beef Stroganoff
- South African Bobotie
- Jamaican Jerk Chicken
- German Schnitzel
- Canadian Poutine
- Polish Pierogi
- Australian Meat Pie
- Hawaiian Poke Bowl
- Malaysian Laksa
- Swiss Fondue
- Cuban Ropa Vieja
- Filipino Adobo
- Middle Eastern Falafel
- Nigerian Jollof Rice
- Portuguese Bacalhau

- Hungarian Goulash
- Burmese Mohinga
- Colombian Arepas
- Caribbean Callaloo
- Pakistani Nihari
- Danish Smørrebrød
- Chilean Pastel de Choclo
- Finnish Salmon Soup
- Indonesian Nasi Goreng
- Belgian Moules-Frites
- Tunisian Shakshuka
- Irish Shepherd's Pie
- Mongolian Beef
- Saudi Kabsa
- Dutch Stamppot

Moroccan Chicken Tagine

Ingredients:

Chicken:

- 4 chicken thighs and/or drumsticks (bone-in, skin-on for flavor)

Spices:

- 2 tsp ground cinnamon
- 1 tsp ground ginger
- 1 tsp ground turmeric
- 1 tsp ground cumin
- 1 tsp paprika
- ½ tsp ground coriander
- Salt and black pepper to taste

Vegetables & Aromatics:

- 1 large onion, finely sliced
- 3 garlic cloves, minced
- 2 medium carrots, peeled and sliced
- 1 cup cherry tomatoes or 2 large tomatoes, chopped

Dried Fruits:

- ½ cup dried apricots, chopped
- ¼ cup golden raisins

Broth & Add-Ins:

- 1 cup chicken broth
- 1 tbsp honey
- 1 preserved lemon (rinsed and chopped, optional but authentic)
- 1 cup green olives

Garnish:

- Fresh cilantro or parsley, chopped
- Toasted almonds or pine nuts (optional)

Other:

- 2 tbsp olive oil

Directions:

1. Prepare the Spice Mix:
In a small bowl, mix all the spices (cinnamon, ginger, turmeric, cumin, paprika, coriander, salt, and pepper).

2. Brown the Chicken:
Heat olive oil in a large tagine or Dutch oven over medium heat. Rub the spice mix over the chicken pieces and sear them for 2-3 minutes on each side until golden. Remove and set aside.

3. Sauté Aromatics:
Add onions and garlic to the same pot, stirring until softened and fragrant, about 5 minutes.

4. Build the Tagine Base:
Add carrots, tomatoes, dried apricots, and raisins to the pot. Stir for 1-2 minutes to combine.

5. Add Chicken and Broth:
Nestle the chicken back into the pot. Pour in the chicken broth and drizzle honey over the mixture.

6. Simmer Slowly:
Reduce the heat to low, cover, and cook for 1 hour. Stir occasionally and add a bit more broth if needed to prevent sticking.

7. Final Additions:
In the last 15 minutes of cooking, stir in preserved lemons and olives. Let the flavors meld.

8. Garnish and Serve:
Remove from heat. Garnish with fresh cilantro or parsley and sprinkle with nuts if using.

Italian Margherita Pizza

Ingredients:

- 1 ball of pizza dough (store-bought or homemade)
- 1 cup canned San Marzano tomatoes, crushed
- 1 tbsp olive oil
- 1 tsp dried oregano
- 8 oz fresh mozzarella, sliced
- Fresh basil leaves
- Salt to taste

Directions:

1. Preheat your oven to 475°F (250°C). If using a pizza stone, place it in the oven to preheat as well.
2. Roll out the dough on a floured surface into a thin circle.
3. Spread the crushed tomatoes over the dough, leaving a small border around the edges. Sprinkle with oregano and a pinch of salt.
4. Add the mozzarella slices evenly over the pizza.
5. Transfer the pizza to the oven and bake for 8-10 minutes, until the crust is golden and the cheese is bubbling.
6. Remove from the oven and garnish with fresh basil leaves and a drizzle of olive oil before serving.

Japanese Ramen Bowl

Ingredients:

- 2 cups chicken or vegetable broth
- 2 tbsp soy sauce
- 1 tbsp miso paste
- 1 tsp sesame oil
- 1 clove garlic, minced
- 1-inch piece of ginger, grated
- 2 packs fresh ramen noodles
- 2 boiled eggs, halved
- 1 cup sliced shiitake mushrooms
- 1 cup chopped bok choy
- Sliced green onions and nori sheets for garnish

Directions:

1. In a pot, heat sesame oil and sauté garlic and ginger until fragrant.
2. Add the broth, soy sauce, and miso paste. Stir until combined and bring to a simmer.
3. Add the mushrooms and bok choy, cooking for 5-7 minutes until tender.
4. Cook the ramen noodles according to the package instructions and divide them into bowls.
5. Pour the hot broth over the noodles.
6. Top each bowl with boiled egg halves, green onions, and a piece of nori. Serve hot.

Mexican Street Tacos

Ingredients:

- 1 lb beef, chicken, or pork, thinly sliced
- 1 tbsp olive oil
- 2 tsp chili powder
- 1 tsp cumin
- 1 tsp smoked paprika
- ½ tsp garlic powder
- 8 small corn tortillas
- 1 cup chopped onion
- 1 cup chopped cilantro
- Lime wedges for serving

Directions:

1. Heat olive oil in a skillet over medium heat.
2. Toss the meat with chili powder, cumin, smoked paprika, and garlic powder. Cook in the skillet until fully cooked, about 6-8 minutes.
3. Warm the corn tortillas in a dry skillet or directly over a flame.
4. Fill each tortilla with the cooked meat, then top with chopped onion and cilantro.
5. Serve with lime wedges on the side.

Indian Butter Chicken

Ingredients:

- 1 lb chicken breasts or thighs, cut into bite-sized pieces
- 2 tbsp butter
- 1 onion, chopped
- 3 garlic cloves, minced
- 1-inch piece of ginger, grated
- 1 can (14 oz) crushed tomatoes
- 1 cup heavy cream
- 2 tbsp garam masala
- 1 tsp turmeric
- 1 tsp paprika
- 1 tsp ground cumin
- Salt and pepper to taste
- Fresh cilantro for garnish

Directions:

1. In a large pan, melt butter over medium heat. Add chopped onion, garlic, and ginger, cooking until softened.
2. Add the chicken pieces and cook until browned on all sides.
3. Stir in the garam masala, turmeric, paprika, and cumin. Cook for another minute.
4. Pour in the crushed tomatoes and bring to a simmer. Let cook for 10 minutes.
5. Stir in the heavy cream and simmer for an additional 10 minutes until the sauce thickens.
6. Garnish with fresh cilantro and serve with rice or naan.

Greek Moussaka

Ingredients:

- 2 eggplants, sliced into 1/4-inch rounds
- 1 lb ground lamb or beef
- 1 onion, chopped
- 2 garlic cloves, minced
- 1 can (14 oz) crushed tomatoes
- 1 tsp ground cinnamon
- 1 tsp dried oregano
- 1/2 cup red wine
- 2 tbsp olive oil
- Salt and pepper to taste
- 1 cup béchamel sauce (made with butter, flour, milk, and nutmeg)

Directions:

1. Preheat the oven to 375°F (190°C).
2. Grill or roast the eggplant slices until tender and browned. Set aside.
3. In a skillet, heat olive oil and cook the onion and garlic until soft. Add the ground meat and cook until browned.
4. Stir in the crushed tomatoes, cinnamon, oregano, red wine, salt, and pepper. Simmer for 20 minutes.
5. In a baking dish, layer the eggplant slices, then top with the meat sauce, followed by a layer of béchamel sauce.
6. Repeat layers and finish with béchamel sauce on top. Bake for 45 minutes until golden brown and bubbly.

French Coq au Vin

Ingredients:

- 1 whole chicken, cut into pieces
- 2 tbsp olive oil
- 1 onion, chopped
- 2 carrots, chopped
- 3 garlic cloves, minced
- 1 cup red wine
- 1 cup chicken broth
- 2 tbsp tomato paste
- 1 tbsp fresh thyme
- 2 bay leaves
- 1/2 cup pearl onions, peeled
- 1/2 cup mushrooms, sliced
- Salt and pepper to taste

Directions:

1. In a large Dutch oven, heat olive oil over medium heat. Brown the chicken pieces on all sides and set aside.
2. Add onion, carrots, and garlic to the pot, cooking until softened.
3. Stir in the tomato paste, followed by the red wine, chicken broth, thyme, and bay leaves.
4. Return the chicken to the pot, add the pearl onions and mushrooms. Bring to a simmer.
5. Cover and cook for 1 hour, stirring occasionally.
6. Season with salt and pepper, and serve with mashed potatoes or crusty bread.

Thai Green Curry

Ingredients:

- 1 lb chicken, beef, or tofu, cut into bite-sized pieces
- 2 tbsp green curry paste
- 1 can (14 oz) coconut milk
- 1 tbsp fish sauce
- 1 tbsp brown sugar
- 1 red bell pepper, sliced
- 1 zucchini, sliced
- 1/2 cup Thai basil leaves
- 1 tbsp lime juice
- Cooked jasmine rice for serving

Directions:

1. In a large pan, cook the chicken or tofu with the green curry paste over medium heat until browned.
2. Add the coconut milk, fish sauce, and brown sugar. Bring to a simmer.
3. Stir in the bell pepper and zucchini, cooking for 5-7 minutes until tender.
4. Add Thai basil leaves and lime juice, stirring until fragrant.
5. Serve over jasmine rice.

Korean Bibimbap

Ingredients:

- 2 cups cooked rice
- 1/2 lb ground beef or chicken
- 1 carrot, julienned
- 1 zucchini, julienned
- 1 cup spinach, blanched
- 1 egg (fried or poached)
- 2 tbsp sesame oil
- 2 tbsp soy sauce
- 1 tbsp gochujang (Korean chili paste)
- 1 tbsp rice vinegar
- 1 tsp sugar
- Sesame seeds for garnish

Directions:

1. In a skillet, cook the ground meat with sesame oil, soy sauce, and gochujang until browned.
2. In a separate pan, sauté the carrot, zucchini, and spinach with a little sesame oil until tender.
3. In each bowl, place a serving of rice, then arrange the vegetables and meat on top.
4. Top with a fried egg and drizzle with sesame oil, soy sauce, and rice vinegar.
5. Garnish with sesame seeds and serve.

Spanish Paella

Ingredients:

- 1 lb chicken, cut into pieces
- 1/2 lb shrimp, peeled and deveined
- 1/2 lb mussels, scrubbed
- 1/2 lb chorizo, sliced
- 2 cups Arborio rice
- 1 onion, chopped
- 2 garlic cloves, minced
- 1 red bell pepper, chopped
- 1 can (14 oz) diced tomatoes
- 4 cups chicken broth
- 1/2 tsp saffron threads
- 1 tsp paprika
- 2 tbsp olive oil
- Lemon wedges for garnish

Directions:

1. Heat olive oil in a large skillet or paella pan. Brown the chicken, chorizo, and shrimp, then set aside.
2. In the same pan, sauté the onion, garlic, and bell pepper until softened.
3. Add the rice, saffron, paprika, and diced tomatoes. Stir to combine.
4. Pour in the chicken broth, bring to a simmer, and cook until the rice is tender, about 20 minutes.
5. Add the cooked chicken, shrimp, and mussels back to the pan. Cook for an additional 10 minutes until everything is heated through.
6. Garnish with lemon wedges before serving.

Vietnamese Pho

Ingredients:

- 1 lb beef brisket or chicken
- 1 onion, halved
- 1-inch piece of ginger, halved
- 4 cups beef or chicken broth
- 1 cinnamon stick
- 3 cloves
- 1 star anise
- 1 tbsp fish sauce
- 1 tbsp soy sauce
- 1 tsp sugar
- Rice noodles (bánh phở)
- Fresh herbs (cilantro, Thai basil)
- Bean sprouts, lime wedges, and jalapeños for garnish

Directions:

1. Char the onion and ginger under a broiler or on an open flame.
2. In a large pot, add the broth, cinnamon stick, cloves, star anise, fish sauce, soy sauce, and sugar. Bring to a simmer.
3. Add the beef or chicken and cook until tender, about 1 hour for beef or 30 minutes for chicken.
4. Cook the rice noodles according to package instructions.
5. Remove the meat and slice thinly.
6. To serve, place noodles in bowls, top with the sliced meat, and pour hot broth over. Garnish with fresh herbs, bean sprouts, lime, and jalapeños.

Chinese Kung Pao Chicken

Ingredients:

- 1 lb chicken breasts, diced
- 2 tbsp soy sauce
- 1 tbsp rice vinegar
- 1 tbsp sugar
- 1 tsp cornstarch
- 2 tbsp vegetable oil
- 1/2 cup roasted peanuts
- 1/2 cup dried red chili peppers
- 1 bell pepper, chopped
- 2 garlic cloves, minced
- 1-inch piece of ginger, minced

Directions:

1. In a bowl, mix the soy sauce, rice vinegar, sugar, and cornstarch. Add the chicken and marinate for 20 minutes.
2. Heat oil in a wok over high heat. Stir-fry the chicken until browned, then remove and set aside.
3. In the same wok, add dried chilies, garlic, and ginger, stir-frying until fragrant.
4. Add the bell pepper and cooked chicken, then stir in the peanuts and sauce mixture.
5. Cook for 2-3 minutes until the sauce thickens.
6. Serve with steamed rice.

Ethiopian Doro Wat

Ingredients:

- 2 lbs chicken drumsticks or thighs
- 2 large onions, chopped
- 4 garlic cloves, minced
- 1-inch piece of ginger, grated
- 1/4 cup niter kibbeh (Ethiopian spiced clarified butter)
- 3 tbsp berbere spice mix
- 1 can (14 oz) crushed tomatoes
- 1 tbsp tomato paste
- 1/2 cup chicken broth
- 6 hard-boiled eggs, peeled
- Salt and pepper to taste
- Injera (Ethiopian flatbread) for serving

Directions:

1. In a large pot, melt the niter kibbeh over medium heat. Add onions, garlic, and ginger, sautéing until softened.
2. Stir in berbere spice mix, cooking for 2 minutes.
3. Add the crushed tomatoes, tomato paste, chicken broth, salt, and pepper. Bring to a simmer.
4. Add the chicken pieces and cook for 45-60 minutes until tender, stirring occasionally.
5. Add the hard-boiled eggs in the last 10 minutes of cooking.
6. Serve hot with injera.

Brazilian Feijoada

Ingredients:

- 1 lb pork shoulder, cubed
- 1/2 lb chorizo or sausage, sliced
- 1/2 lb smoked sausage, sliced
- 1 lb black beans, soaked overnight
- 1 onion, chopped
- 4 garlic cloves, minced
- 2 bay leaves
- 1 tbsp paprika
- 1 tsp cumin
- 1/2 tsp black pepper
- 4 cups chicken broth
- 1 orange, peeled and sliced
- 2 tbsp olive oil
- Fresh cilantro for garnish
- Steamed rice for serving

Directions:

1. In a large pot, heat olive oil over medium heat. Brown the pork shoulder and sausages.
2. Add onions and garlic, cooking until softened.
3. Stir in black beans, bay leaves, paprika, cumin, and pepper. Add chicken broth and orange slices.
4. Bring to a boil, reduce to a simmer, and cook for 1.5 to 2 hours until the beans are tender.
5. Serve with steamed rice and garnish with fresh cilantro.

Turkish Kebab

Ingredients:

- 1 lb ground lamb or beef
- 1 onion, finely grated
- 2 garlic cloves, minced
- 1 tbsp cumin
- 1 tsp paprika
- 1/2 tsp ground cinnamon
- Salt and black pepper to taste
- 1 tbsp olive oil
- Fresh parsley for garnish
- Pita bread or flatbreads for serving

Directions:

1. In a bowl, mix ground meat, grated onion, garlic, cumin, paprika, cinnamon, salt, and pepper until well combined.
2. Shape the mixture into kebabs and thread onto skewers.
3. Heat olive oil in a grill pan over medium-high heat. Cook kebabs for 4-5 minutes on each side until browned and cooked through.
4. Garnish with fresh parsley and serve with pita bread.

American Barbecue Ribs

Ingredients:

- 2 racks baby back ribs
- 2 tbsp brown sugar
- 1 tbsp paprika
- 1 tsp garlic powder
- 1 tsp onion powder
- 1 tsp chili powder
- Salt and pepper to taste
- 1 cup barbecue sauce
- 1 tbsp olive oil

Directions:

1. Preheat oven to 300°F (150°C).
2. Remove the membrane from the ribs and rub with olive oil.
3. Mix brown sugar, paprika, garlic powder, onion powder, chili powder, salt, and pepper. Rub the spice mix all over the ribs.
4. Wrap the ribs in foil and bake for 2.5-3 hours.
5. Unwrap the ribs, brush with barbecue sauce, and grill or broil for 5-10 minutes until caramelized.
6. Serve with extra barbecue sauce.

Argentinian Empanadas

Ingredients:

- 1 lb ground beef
- 1 onion, chopped
- 1/2 cup green olives, chopped
- 1/4 cup raisins
- 2 hard-boiled eggs, chopped
- 1 tsp cumin
- 1/2 tsp paprika
- Salt and pepper to taste
- 1 package empanada dough discs
- Olive oil for frying

Directions:

1. In a skillet, cook ground beef and onion until browned.
2. Stir in cumin, paprika, olives, raisins, hard-boiled eggs, salt, and pepper. Cook for 5 minutes.
3. Remove from heat and let the filling cool.
4. Place a spoonful of filling on each empanada dough disc. Fold and seal the edges.
5. Heat olive oil in a skillet and fry the empanadas until golden brown.
6. Serve hot.

Lebanese Tabouleh

Ingredients:

- 1 cup bulgur wheat
- 1 1/2 cups boiling water
- 2 tomatoes, diced
- 1 cucumber, diced
- 1 bunch parsley, finely chopped
- 1/2 bunch mint, finely chopped
- 1/4 cup olive oil
- 2 tbsp lemon juice
- Salt and pepper to taste

Directions:

1. Place bulgur wheat in a bowl and pour boiling water over it. Let it sit for 15 minutes to soften.
2. Fluff the bulgur with a fork, then stir in tomatoes, cucumber, parsley, and mint.
3. Drizzle with olive oil and lemon juice, season with salt and pepper, and toss to combine.
4. Serve chilled as a side dish.

Swedish Meatballs

Ingredients:

- 1 lb ground beef
- 1/2 lb ground pork
- 1/2 onion, finely chopped
- 1/4 cup breadcrumbs
- 1 egg
- 1/2 cup milk
- 1 tsp allspice
- 1 tsp salt
- 1/2 tsp black pepper
- 2 tbsp butter
- 2 tbsp flour
- 2 cups beef broth
- 1/2 cup heavy cream

Directions:

1. In a bowl, combine beef, pork, onion, breadcrumbs, egg, milk, allspice, salt, and pepper.
2. Shape the mixture into small meatballs.
3. In a skillet, melt butter over medium heat and brown the meatballs on all sides.
4. Remove the meatballs and set aside. In the same skillet, add flour and cook for 1 minute.
5. Gradually add beef broth and bring to a simmer. Add the meatballs back into the skillet.
6. Stir in the heavy cream and cook for 10 minutes until the sauce thickens.
7. Serve with mashed potatoes or lingonberry sauce.

Peruvian Ceviche

Ingredients:

- 1 lb fresh white fish (such as tilapia or sea bass), diced
- 1 red onion, thinly sliced
- 1-2 fresh chili peppers, minced
- 1/2 cup fresh lime juice
- 1/4 cup fresh lemon juice
- 1/2 cup cilantro, chopped
- 1 tsp salt
- 1/2 tsp pepper
- 1 sweet potato, boiled and sliced (optional)
- Corn kernels for garnish (optional)

Directions:

1. In a bowl, combine diced fish, onion, and chili peppers.
2. Pour lime and lemon juice over the mixture and stir gently.
3. Let the ceviche sit for 15-20 minutes until the fish is opaque.
4. Stir in cilantro, salt, and pepper.
5. Serve with slices of boiled sweet potato and garnish with corn if desired.

Russian Beef Stroganoff

Ingredients:

- 1 lb beef sirloin or tenderloin, cut into thin strips
- 2 tbsp butter
- 1 onion, finely chopped
- 2 garlic cloves, minced
- 1 cup mushrooms, sliced
- 1 tbsp flour
- 1 cup beef broth
- 1 cup sour cream
- 1 tbsp Dijon mustard
- Salt and pepper to taste
- Fresh parsley for garnish
- Egg noodles or rice for serving

Directions:

1. In a skillet, melt butter over medium-high heat. Add beef strips and cook until browned. Remove and set aside.
2. In the same skillet, sauté onions, garlic, and mushrooms until softened.
3. Stir in flour and cook for 1 minute.
4. Gradually add beef broth, stirring until the mixture thickens.
5. Stir in sour cream and Dijon mustard. Return the beef to the skillet and simmer for 5 minutes.
6. Season with salt and pepper to taste.
7. Serve over egg noodles or rice, garnished with fresh parsley.

South African Bobotie

Ingredients:

- 1 lb ground beef or lamb
- 1 onion, chopped
- 2 garlic cloves, minced
- 1 tbsp curry powder
- 1 tsp turmeric
- 1 tsp ground cumin
- 1 tbsp sugar
- 1/2 cup raisins
- 1/4 cup sliced almonds
- 2 slices white bread, soaked in milk
- 1/2 cup milk
- 2 eggs
- 1 tbsp vinegar
- Salt and pepper to taste
- Fresh cilantro for garnish

Directions:

1. Preheat oven to 350°F (175°C).
2. In a pan, sauté onions and garlic until soft. Add ground beef or lamb and cook until browned.
3. Stir in curry powder, turmeric, cumin, sugar, raisins, and almonds.
4. Squeeze excess milk from soaked bread and crumble into the mixture.
5. Transfer to a baking dish.
6. In a bowl, whisk together milk, eggs, vinegar, salt, and pepper. Pour over the meat mixture.
7. Bake for 30-40 minutes until golden.
8. Garnish with fresh cilantro and serve with rice.

Jamaican Jerk Chicken

Ingredients:

- 4 chicken thighs or drumsticks
- 1/4 cup soy sauce
- 1/4 cup olive oil
- 1 onion, chopped
- 2 garlic cloves, minced
- 1 tbsp fresh thyme, chopped
- 2 tbsp brown sugar
- 1 tbsp allspice
- 1 tsp cinnamon
- 1 tsp nutmeg
- 1 scotch bonnet pepper, chopped (or substitute with jalapeño)
- Salt and pepper to taste

Directions:

1. In a blender, combine soy sauce, olive oil, onion, garlic, thyme, sugar, allspice, cinnamon, nutmeg, scotch bonnet pepper, salt, and pepper. Blend until smooth.
2. Marinate chicken in the jerk marinade for at least 2 hours, or overnight for more flavor.
3. Preheat grill to medium-high heat. Grill chicken for 6-8 minutes per side, until cooked through.
4. Serve with rice and peas.

German Schnitzel

Ingredients:

- 4 boneless pork or veal cutlets
- 1 cup all-purpose flour
- 2 large eggs, beaten
- 1 cup breadcrumbs
- 1 tbsp paprika
- Salt and pepper to taste
- 4 tbsp butter
- Lemon wedges for garnish

Directions:

1. Tenderize the meat using a mallet until thin.
2. Season the flour with paprika, salt, and pepper. Dip each cutlet into flour, then eggs, and finally breadcrumbs.
3. In a skillet, heat butter over medium-high heat. Fry each schnitzel for 3-4 minutes per side until golden brown.
4. Drain on paper towels and serve with lemon wedges.

Canadian Poutine

Ingredients:

- 4 cups French fries (fresh or frozen)
- 1 1/2 cups cheese curds
- 2 cups beef gravy

Directions:

1. Cook French fries according to package directions or deep fry until crispy.
2. Heat beef gravy in a saucepan until simmering.
3. Place hot fries on a plate or dish. Top with cheese curds, then pour gravy over.
4. Serve immediately and enjoy!

Polish Pierogi

Ingredients:

Dough:

- 2 cups all-purpose flour
- 1 egg
- 1/2 cup sour cream
- 1/4 cup butter, softened
- 1/2 tsp salt

Filling:

- 1 cup mashed potatoes
- 1/2 cup cooked and crumbled bacon
- 1/2 cup sautéed onions
- Salt and pepper to taste

Directions:

1. For the dough, combine flour, egg, sour cream, butter, and salt in a bowl. Knead until smooth, then cover and let rest for 30 minutes.
2. For the filling, mix mashed potatoes, bacon, onions, salt, and pepper.
3. Roll out the dough and cut into circles. Place a spoonful of filling on each circle, fold, and seal the edges.
4. Boil pierogi in salted water for 3-4 minutes until they float to the top.
5. Optionally, sauté cooked pierogi in butter until golden. Serve with sour cream.

Australian Meat Pie

Ingredients:

- 1 lb ground beef
- 1 onion, chopped
- 1 carrot, diced
- 1/2 cup beef broth
- 1 tbsp tomato paste
- 1 tsp Worcestershire sauce
- 1 tsp paprika
- 1/2 tsp thyme
- 1 package puff pastry (for top and bottom)
- 1 egg, beaten

Directions:

1. Preheat oven to 400°F (200°C).
2. In a skillet, cook ground beef and onion until browned. Add carrot, beef broth, tomato paste, Worcestershire sauce, paprika, thyme, salt, and pepper. Simmer for 10 minutes.
3. Roll out puff pastry and line a pie dish. Fill with the meat mixture, then cover with another layer of pastry.
4. Seal edges and cut slits in the top. Brush with beaten egg.
5. Bake for 25-30 minutes until golden brown.

Hawaiian Poke Bowl

Ingredients:

- 1 lb sushi-grade tuna, diced
- 1/4 cup soy sauce
- 1 tbsp sesame oil
- 1 tsp rice vinegar
- 1/2 tsp chili flakes (optional)
- 1 avocado, sliced
- 1 cucumber, sliced
- 1 cup cooked rice (white, brown, or sushi rice)
- 1 tbsp sesame seeds
- 2 tbsp green onions, chopped

Directions:

1. In a bowl, mix soy sauce, sesame oil, rice vinegar, chili flakes, and diced tuna. Let marinate for 10-15 minutes.
2. Serve over a bowl of rice, topped with avocado, cucumber, and marinated tuna.
3. Garnish with sesame seeds and green onions. Enjoy!

Malaysian Laksa

Ingredients:

- 2 tbsp vegetable oil
- 1 onion, chopped
- 3 garlic cloves, minced
- 1-inch piece of ginger, minced
- 1 tbsp red curry paste
- 1 can (400ml) coconut milk
- 4 cups chicken broth
- 2 tbsp fish sauce
- 1 tbsp sugar
- 1 lb cooked chicken breast or shrimp
- 2 oz rice noodles, cooked
- 2 boiled eggs, halved
- 1/2 cup bean sprouts
- 1/4 cup cilantro, chopped
- 2 spring onions, chopped
- 1 lime, cut into wedges
- Red chili slices for garnish (optional)

Directions:

1. Heat vegetable oil in a large pot over medium heat. Sauté onion, garlic, and ginger until softened, about 5 minutes.
2. Stir in red curry paste and cook for 1-2 minutes until fragrant.
3. Add coconut milk, chicken broth, fish sauce, and sugar. Bring to a simmer and cook for 10 minutes.
4. Add cooked chicken or shrimp to the broth and heat through.
5. To serve, divide rice noodles into bowls. Pour hot soup over the noodles.
6. Garnish with boiled eggs, bean sprouts, cilantro, spring onions, lime wedges, and chili slices. Serve immediately.

Swiss Fondue

Ingredients:

- 8 oz Gruyère cheese, grated
- 8 oz Emmental cheese, grated
- 1 clove garlic, halved
- 1 1/2 cups dry white wine
- 1 tbsp lemon juice
- 1 tsp cornstarch
- 2 tbsp kirsch (cherry brandy) or water
- Freshly ground black pepper
- Freshly grated nutmeg
- 1 French baguette, cubed

Directions:

1. Rub the inside of a fondue pot with the garlic halves.
2. In a medium bowl, toss the grated cheeses with cornstarch.
3. Pour wine and lemon juice into the fondue pot over medium heat.
4. Gradually add the cheese mixture, stirring constantly until melted and smooth.
5. Stir in kirsch, black pepper, and nutmeg.
6. Serve with cubed bread for dipping.
7. Keep the fondue warm on a low heat as you dip the bread cubes.

Cuban Ropa Vieja

Ingredients:

- 2 lbs flank steak or skirt steak
- 1 onion, sliced
- 1 bell pepper, sliced
- 3 garlic cloves, minced
- 1 (14.5 oz) can diced tomatoes
- 1/2 cup dry white wine
- 2 tbsp olive oil
- 1 tsp cumin
- 1 tsp paprika
- 1/2 tsp oregano
- 1/4 tsp red pepper flakes
- 1/4 cup green olives, pitted and sliced
- 2 tbsp capers
- 1/4 cup fresh cilantro, chopped
- Salt and pepper to taste
- Rice for serving

Directions:

1. In a large pot, heat olive oil over medium-high heat. Brown the steak on both sides. Remove and set aside.
2. In the same pot, sauté onions, bell pepper, and garlic until softened.
3. Add diced tomatoes, wine, cumin, paprika, oregano, and red pepper flakes. Stir and return the steak to the pot.
4. Cover with water, bring to a boil, then reduce to a simmer and cook for 2-3 hours until the meat is tender and shreds easily.
5. Shred the meat and return it to the sauce, adding olives and capers. Simmer for another 10-15 minutes.
6. Garnish with cilantro and serve with rice.

Filipino Adobo

Ingredients:

- 2 lbs chicken thighs or pork belly, cut into chunks
- 1/2 cup soy sauce
- 1/4 cup vinegar
- 1 onion, chopped
- 6 garlic cloves, minced
- 2 bay leaves
- 1 tsp whole black peppercorns
- 1 tbsp brown sugar (optional)
- Salt and pepper to taste
- 2 tbsp vegetable oil
- 1 cup water

Directions:

1. In a bowl, combine soy sauce, vinegar, onion, garlic, bay leaves, peppercorns, and brown sugar. Add the meat and marinate for 30 minutes to 1 hour.
2. Heat vegetable oil in a large pot over medium heat. Add the marinated meat and cook until browned on all sides.
3. Add water and bring to a simmer. Cover and cook for 45 minutes, stirring occasionally.
4. Once the meat is tender, remove the cover and simmer for another 15 minutes to reduce the sauce.
5. Season with salt and pepper to taste and serve with steamed rice.

Middle Eastern Falafel

Ingredients:

- 2 cups dried chickpeas (soaked overnight)
- 1 onion, chopped
- 4 garlic cloves, minced
- 1 cup fresh parsley, chopped
- 1 cup fresh cilantro, chopped
- 2 tsp ground cumin
- 2 tsp ground coriander
- 1 tsp salt
- 1/2 tsp black pepper
- 1/2 tsp baking soda
- 1/4 cup flour (more if needed)
- Vegetable oil for frying

Directions:

1. Drain and rinse the soaked chickpeas.
2. In a food processor, pulse the chickpeas, onion, garlic, parsley, cilantro, cumin, coriander, salt, and pepper until coarse.
3. Sprinkle the mixture with baking soda, add flour, and pulse until combined. Let the dough rest for 30 minutes.
4. Shape the mixture into small balls or patties.
5. Heat oil in a deep frying pan over medium-high heat. Fry falafel in batches for 3-4 minutes until golden brown.
6. Drain on paper towels and serve with pita, tahini, or yogurt sauce.

Nigerian Jollof Rice

Ingredients:

- 2 cups long-grain parboiled rice
- 2 tbsp vegetable oil
- 1 onion, chopped
- 2 garlic cloves, minced
- 1 bell pepper, chopped
- 1 can (14.5 oz) diced tomatoes
- 2 tbsp tomato paste
- 1 tsp ground thyme
- 1 tsp curry powder
- 1 tsp paprika
- 1/2 tsp cayenne pepper (optional)
- 2 cups chicken broth
- 1/4 cup green peas (optional)
- Salt to taste

Directions:

1. Wash the rice under cold water and set aside.
2. In a large pot, heat vegetable oil and sauté onion, garlic, and bell pepper until softened.
3. Add diced tomatoes, tomato paste, thyme, curry powder, paprika, and cayenne pepper. Simmer for 10 minutes.
4. Add chicken broth and bring to a boil. Stir in the rice, cover, and reduce heat to low.
5. Cook for 20-25 minutes, until the rice is tender and liquid is absorbed.
6. Optional: Add green peas and cook for an additional 5 minutes. Fluff the rice and serve.

Portuguese Bacalhau

Ingredients:

- 1 lb salted cod (bacalhau), soaked and flaked
- 1/4 cup olive oil
- 1 onion, sliced
- 4 garlic cloves, minced
- 2 medium potatoes, thinly sliced
- 1/2 cup black olives, pitted
- 1/4 cup fresh parsley, chopped
- 1/2 tsp paprika
- Salt and pepper to taste

Directions:

1. Preheat oven to 350°F (175°C).
2. In a skillet, heat olive oil and sauté onions and garlic until softened.
3. In a greased baking dish, layer sliced potatoes, followed by cod, onions, and garlic.
4. Sprinkle paprika, olives, and parsley on top. Drizzle with olive oil.
5. Cover with foil and bake for 30-40 minutes until potatoes are tender.
6. Remove from oven, season with salt and pepper, and serve.

Hungarian Goulash

Ingredients:

- 2 tbsp vegetable oil
- 1 lb beef chuck, cut into cubes
- 1 onion, chopped
- 2 garlic cloves, minced
- 2 tbsp paprika
- 1 tsp caraway seeds
- 2 medium potatoes, cubed
- 2 carrots, chopped
- 1 bell pepper, chopped
- 1 can (14.5 oz) diced tomatoes
- 3 cups beef broth
- Salt and pepper to taste

Directions:

1. Heat oil in a large pot over medium-high heat. Brown the beef cubes on all sides.
2. Add onions and garlic, and cook until softened. Stir in paprika and caraway seeds.
3. Add potatoes, carrots, bell pepper, diced tomatoes, and beef broth. Bring to a boil.
4. Reduce heat, cover, and simmer for 1-1.5 hours until the beef is tender.
5. Season with salt and pepper and serve hot.

Burmese Mohinga

Ingredients:

- 2 tbsp vegetable oil
- 1 onion, chopped
- 2 garlic cloves, minced
- 1-inch piece of ginger, minced
- 2 stalks lemongrass, smashed
- 1 tbsp turmeric
- 2 cups fish stock
- 1 can (400ml) coconut milk
- 1 lb catfish fillets (or any white fish), cut into pieces
- 1 tbsp fish sauce
- 1 tbsp tamarind paste
- 2 tbsp rice flour (optional, for thickening)
- 1/2 tsp sugar
- 1/2 cup cilantro, chopped
- 1/4 cup green onions, chopped
- 1/4 cup boiled eggs, chopped (optional)
- 1 lime, cut into wedges
- 1 tbsp fried garlic or shallots (for garnish)
- 1-2 cups cooked rice noodles

Directions:

1. Heat vegetable oil in a large pot over medium heat. Add onion, garlic, ginger, and lemongrass. Sauté until fragrant.
2. Stir in turmeric, fish stock, and coconut milk. Bring to a simmer and cook for 10 minutes.
3. Add fish pieces, fish sauce, tamarind paste, rice flour (if using), and sugar. Let it cook for 10-15 minutes until the fish is tender.
4. Remove from heat and discard the lemongrass.
5. To serve, place cooked noodles in bowls and ladle the soup over them.
6. Garnish with cilantro, green onions, boiled egg, lime wedges, and fried garlic.

Colombian Arepas

Ingredients:

- 2 cups arepa flour (masarepa)
- 2 cups warm water
- 1 tsp salt
- 1 tbsp butter (optional)
- 1/2 cup shredded cheese (optional)
- Vegetable oil for frying

Directions:

1. In a large bowl, mix the arepa flour, salt, and warm water. Stir until a dough forms. Let it rest for 5 minutes.
2. Divide the dough into small balls, then flatten them into discs about 1/2 inch thick.
3. Optionally, fold cheese into the center before flattening.
4. Heat a little vegetable oil in a skillet over medium heat. Fry the arepas for 4-5 minutes on each side until golden brown.
5. Remove from heat and serve warm with butter or toppings like cheese or avocado.

Caribbean Callaloo

Ingredients:

- 1 lb fresh callaloo leaves (or spinach as a substitute)
- 2 tbsp vegetable oil
- 1 onion, chopped
- 2 garlic cloves, minced
- 1 bell pepper, chopped
- 1 tomato, chopped
- 1/2 cup coconut milk
- 1/2 tsp thyme
- 1/4 tsp scotch bonnet pepper (or to taste)
- Salt and pepper to taste
- 1/2 cup cooked salted cod (optional)
- 1/4 cup green onions, chopped

Directions:

1. Heat oil in a large pot and sauté onions, garlic, bell pepper, and tomato until soft.
2. Add the callaloo leaves (or spinach), coconut milk, thyme, and scotch bonnet pepper. Cook until the leaves are wilted.
3. Stir in the salted cod (if using) and cook for an additional 5 minutes.
4. Season with salt and pepper to taste and garnish with green onions.
5. Serve with rice or as a side dish to any main course.

Pakistani Nihari

Ingredients:

- 1 lb beef shank or stew meat, cut into chunks
- 2 tbsp vegetable oil
- 2 onions, thinly sliced
- 4 garlic cloves, minced
- 1-inch piece of ginger, minced
- 2 tbsp ground coriander
- 2 tbsp ground cumin
- 1 tbsp ground turmeric
- 1 tbsp ground paprika
- 1 cinnamon stick
- 4 cloves
- 4 cardamom pods
- 3 cups beef broth
- 1 tbsp lemon juice
- Salt to taste
- 2 tbsp flour (optional, for thickening)
- Chopped cilantro and ginger for garnish
- Naan or rice for serving

Directions:

1. Heat vegetable oil in a large pot and brown the beef chunks on all sides.
2. Add onions, garlic, and ginger, and cook until softened.
3. Stir in ground coriander, cumin, turmeric, paprika, cinnamon stick, cloves, and cardamom. Cook for 1-2 minutes until fragrant.
4. Add beef broth, bring to a boil, then reduce heat and simmer for 2-3 hours until the meat is tender.
5. If you want to thicken the sauce, mix flour with water to form a slurry, then add it to the pot and cook for an additional 10-15 minutes.
6. Add lemon juice and season with salt.
7. Garnish with cilantro and ginger, and serve with naan or rice.

Danish Smørrebrød

Ingredients:

- 1 loaf rye bread (dense, dark rye)
- 1/2 lb pickled herring, drained
- 1/2 lb roast beef, thinly sliced
- 4 boiled eggs, sliced
- 1 small onion, thinly sliced
- 1/2 cup mayonnaise
- 2 tbsp Dijon mustard
- Fresh dill for garnish
- Salt and pepper to taste

Directions:

1. Slice the rye bread into individual pieces.
2. For the pickled herring version, place a few pieces of herring on each slice of bread, topping with onions and dill.
3. For the roast beef version, spread mayonnaise on the bread, layer with roast beef, top with boiled eggs, and drizzle with mustard.
4. Season each slice with salt, pepper, and fresh dill.
5. Serve as an open-faced sandwich, typically with pickles or salad on the side.

Chilean Pastel de Choclo

Ingredients:

- 4 cups fresh or frozen corn kernels
- 1/2 cup milk
- 1/4 cup butter
- 1/4 cup sugar
- 1 lb ground beef
- 1 onion, chopped
- 2 hard-boiled eggs, chopped
- 1/4 cup black olives, chopped
- 1 tbsp paprika
- 1 tsp cumin
- 1/4 cup raisins (optional)
- 1/4 cup fresh basil, chopped
- Salt and pepper to taste
- 1/4 cup grated Parmesan cheese

Directions:

1. In a blender, blend the corn kernels with milk, butter, and sugar until smooth.
2. In a large skillet, sauté the onion in a little oil until softened. Add ground beef and cook until browned.
3. Stir in paprika, cumin, raisins, and season with salt and pepper.
4. Preheat oven to 350°F (175°C).
5. In a casserole dish, layer the beef mixture, followed by the chopped eggs, olives, and fresh basil.
6. Pour the corn mixture over the top and sprinkle with grated Parmesan cheese.
7. Bake for 25-30 minutes, until golden and bubbly.
8. Serve warm.

Finnish Salmon Soup (Lohikeitto)

Ingredients:

- 1 lb salmon fillets, skin removed and cut into cubes
- 4 cups fish or chicken broth
- 1 cup heavy cream
- 4 medium potatoes, peeled and diced
- 1 onion, chopped
- 2 carrots, sliced
- 1 leek, sliced
- 1 tbsp fresh dill, chopped
- Salt and pepper to taste
- 2 tbsp butter

Directions:

1. In a large pot, melt butter over medium heat. Add onion, leek, carrots, and potatoes, and cook for about 5 minutes.
2. Pour in the broth, bring to a boil, then reduce to a simmer and cook for 15 minutes until the potatoes are tender.
3. Add salmon cubes and cook for an additional 5-7 minutes.
4. Stir in heavy cream and dill. Season with salt and pepper to taste.
5. Serve hot with rye bread on the side.

Indonesian Nasi Goreng

Ingredients:

- 2 cups cooked jasmine rice (preferably day-old)
- 2 tbsp vegetable oil
- 2 garlic cloves, minced
- 1 shallot, chopped
- 1 red chili, chopped
- 1 egg, scrambled
- 1/4 cup cooked chicken or shrimp (optional)
- 2 tbsp soy sauce
- 1 tbsp sweet soy sauce (kecap manis)
- 1/2 tsp ground white pepper
- 1/4 cup green onions, chopped
- 1/4 cup cucumber slices for garnish
- Fried shallots for garnish (optional)

Directions:

1. Heat vegetable oil in a large skillet or wok over medium-high heat. Add garlic, shallot, and red chili. Stir-fry for 1-2 minutes until fragrant.
2. Push the ingredients to one side of the pan and scramble the egg on the other side.
3. Add the cooked rice and break up any clumps. Stir in soy sauce, sweet soy sauce, and white pepper.
4. Add cooked chicken or shrimp (if using) and mix everything together.
5. Garnish with green onions, cucumber slices, and fried shallots.
6. Serve hot as a main or side dish.

Belgian Moules-Frites

Ingredients:

- 2 lbs mussels, cleaned and debearded
- 2 tbsp butter
- 1 onion, finely chopped
- 2 garlic cloves, minced
- 1 cup dry white wine
- 1 cup vegetable broth
- 2 tbsp fresh parsley, chopped
- 1 lemon, cut into wedges
- Salt and pepper to taste
- For the frites:
    - 4 large potatoes, peeled and cut into fries
    - Vegetable oil for frying
    - Salt for seasoning

Directions:

1. Begin by making the frites: Heat vegetable oil in a deep fryer or large pot to 350°F (175°C). Fry the potato fries in batches until golden and crispy. Remove from the oil, drain on paper towels, and season with salt.
2. In a large pot, melt butter over medium heat. Add the chopped onion and garlic, cooking until softened, about 5 minutes.
3. Add the white wine and vegetable broth to the pot, then bring to a simmer.
4. Add the mussels, cover, and cook for 5-7 minutes, or until the mussels have opened. Discard any that do not open.
5. Season with salt, pepper, and freshly chopped parsley.
6. Serve the mussels with lemon wedges and a side of hot frites.

Tunisian Shakshuka

Ingredients:

- 2 tbsp olive oil
- 1 onion, chopped
- 1 red bell pepper, chopped
- 2 garlic cloves, minced
- 2 tsp ground cumin
- 1 tsp ground paprika
- 1/2 tsp ground coriander
- 1/4 tsp ground cayenne pepper
- 1 can (14 oz) crushed tomatoes
- 4 large eggs
- Salt and pepper to taste
- Fresh cilantro, chopped for garnish
- Crusty bread for serving

Directions:

1. Heat olive oil in a large skillet over medium heat. Add the chopped onion and bell pepper. Cook, stirring occasionally, until softened (about 5 minutes).
2. Add the minced garlic and cook for an additional 1-2 minutes. Stir in the cumin, paprika, coriander, and cayenne, cooking until fragrant.
3. Pour in the crushed tomatoes and stir to combine. Let the mixture simmer for about 10 minutes, allowing the sauce to thicken.
4. Using a spoon, make 4 small wells in the sauce. Crack an egg into each well. Cover and cook for 5-7 minutes, or until the eggs are cooked to your desired doneness.
5. Season with salt and pepper to taste, and garnish with fresh cilantro. Serve with crusty bread to scoop up the sauce.

Irish Shepherd's Pie

Ingredients:

- 1 lb ground lamb (or beef for cottage pie)
- 1 onion, chopped
- 2 carrots, diced
- 2 garlic cloves, minced
- 1 cup frozen peas
- 2 tbsp tomato paste
- 1 cup beef broth
- 1 tsp Worcestershire sauce
- 1 tsp dried thyme
- 4 large potatoes, peeled and cubed
- 1/2 cup milk
- 4 tbsp butter
- Salt and pepper to taste

Directions:

1. Preheat the oven to 375°F (190°C).
2. In a large skillet, brown the ground lamb over medium heat. Drain any excess fat.
3. Add the chopped onion, carrots, and garlic to the skillet. Cook until the vegetables are softened, about 5-7 minutes.
4. Stir in the tomato paste, then add the beef broth, Worcestershire sauce, and thyme. Simmer for 10 minutes until the sauce thickens.
5. Meanwhile, cook the potatoes in a large pot of salted boiling water until tender, about 15 minutes. Drain and mash with milk and butter. Season with salt and pepper.
6. Transfer the meat mixture into a baking dish, spreading it evenly. Top with the mashed potatoes, spreading them out to cover the filling completely.
7. Bake for 20 minutes or until the top is golden brown. Serve hot.

Mongolian Beef

Ingredients:

- 1 lb flank steak, thinly sliced
- 2 tbsp cornstarch
- 2 tbsp vegetable oil
- 2 cloves garlic, minced
- 1-inch piece of ginger, minced
- 1/4 cup soy sauce
- 1/4 cup water
- 2 tbsp brown sugar

- 1 tbsp rice vinegar
- 1/2 tsp red pepper flakes (optional)
- 1/4 cup green onions, chopped

Directions:

1. Toss the sliced flank steak in cornstarch until evenly coated.
2. Heat vegetable oil in a large skillet or wok over medium-high heat. Add the beef and cook until browned and crispy, about 3-4 minutes per side. Remove the beef from the pan and set aside.
3. In the same pan, add garlic and ginger, sautéing for 1-2 minutes until fragrant.
4. Add soy sauce, water, brown sugar, rice vinegar, and red pepper flakes (if using). Bring to a simmer and cook for 3-4 minutes, allowing the sauce to thicken.
5. Return the beef to the skillet and toss to coat in the sauce. Cook for an additional 2 minutes.
6. Garnish with chopped green onions and serve with steamed rice.

Saudi Kabsa

Ingredients:

- 2 tbsp vegetable oil
- 1 onion, chopped
- 2 garlic cloves, minced
- 1 tsp ground cumin
- 1 tsp ground coriander
- 1/2 tsp ground turmeric
- 1/2 tsp ground cinnamon
- 1 tsp ground cardamom
- 2 cups basmati rice, rinsed
- 4 cups chicken broth
- 2 lbs chicken pieces (drumsticks or thighs)
- 2 tomatoes, chopped
- 1/2 cup raisins
- 1/4 cup slivered almonds, toasted
- Salt and pepper to taste
- Fresh cilantro for garnish

Directions:

1. Heat vegetable oil in a large pot over medium heat. Add the onion and garlic, cooking until softened.

2. Stir in the cumin, coriander, turmeric, cinnamon, and cardamom, and cook for 1-2 minutes until fragrant.
3. Add the rice, chicken broth, chicken pieces, tomatoes, and raisins. Bring to a boil, then reduce heat to low, cover, and simmer for 25-30 minutes, until the rice is cooked and the chicken is tender.
4. Fluff the rice with a fork and garnish with toasted almonds and fresh cilantro. Serve hot.

Dutch Stamppot

Ingredients:

- 2 lbs potatoes, peeled and cubed
- 1 lb smoked sausage (rookworst), sliced
- 1/2 lb kale or sauerkraut (for boerenkool stamppot or zuurkool stamppot)
- 1/2 cup milk
- 4 tbsp butter
- Salt and pepper to taste

Directions:

1. Boil the potatoes in salted water until tender, about 15 minutes.
2. While the potatoes are cooking, blanch the kale or sauerkraut in a separate pot of boiling water for 3-4 minutes. Drain well.
3. Mash the cooked potatoes with milk and butter, seasoning with salt and pepper.
4. Stir in the kale or sauerkraut until well combined.
5. Serve with sliced smoked sausage on top and additional butter if desired.

www.ingramcontent.com/pod-product-compliance
Lightning Source LLC
LaVergne TN
LVHW081508060526
838201LV00056BA/3007